Night Prayer (Compline)

C000076855

Church House Publishing

Published by   Church House Publishing
                    Church House
                    Great Smith Street
                    London SW1P 3NZ

Copyright ©   *The Archbishops' Council 2000*

                    First published 2000

                    0 7151 2031 X

Printed and bound by ArklePrint Ltd, Northampton
on 80 gsm Dutchman Ivory

Typeset in Gill Sans
by John Morgan and Shirley Thompson/Omnific
Designed by Derek Birdsall RDI

The material in this booklet is extracted from *Common Worship:
Services and Prayers for the Church of England*. It comprises:

¶   An Order for Night Prayer (Compline);
¶   Notes to Night Prayer (Compline).

For other material, page references to *Common Worship:
Services and Prayers for the Church of England* are supplied.

Pagination   This booklet has two sets of page numbers. The outer numbers
              are the booklet's own page numbers, while the inner numbers
              near the centre of most pages refer to the equivalent pages in
              Common Worship: Services and Prayers for the Church of England.

Contents

An Order for Night Prayer (Compline)

Note

The ancient office of Compline derives its name from a Latin word meaning 'completion' (*completorium*). It is above all a service of quietness and reflection before rest at the end of the day. It is most effective when the ending is indeed an ending, without additions, conversation or noise. If there is an address, or business to be done, it should come first. If the service is in church, those present depart in silence; if at home, they go quietly to bed.

For further Notes, see page 9.

An Order for Night Prayer (Compline)

Preparation

The Lord almighty grant us a quiet night and a perfect end.

All **Amen.**

Our help is in the name of the Lord

All **who made heaven and earth.**

A period of silence for reflection on the past day may follow.

The following or other suitable words of penitence may be used

All **Most merciful God,**
we confess to you,
before the whole company of heaven and one another,
that we have sinned in thought, word and deed
and in what we have failed to do.
Forgive us our sins,
heal us by your Spirit
and raise us to new life in Christ. Amen.

O God, make speed to save us.

All **O Lord, make haste to help us.**

All **Glory to the Father and to the Son**
and to the Holy Spirit;
as it was in the beginning is now
and shall be for ever. Amen.
Alleluia.

Before the ending of the day,
Creator of the world, we pray
That you, with steadfast love, would keep
Your watch around us while we sleep.

From evil dreams defend our sight,
From fears and terrors of the night;
Tread underfoot our deadly foe
That we no sinful thought may know.

O Father, that we ask be done
Through Jesus Christ, your only Son;
And Holy Spirit, by whose breath
Our souls are raised to life from death.

The Word of God

Psalmody

One or more of the following psalms may be used.

Psalm 4

1   Answer me when I call, O God of my righteousness; ♦
you set me at liberty when I was in trouble;
     have mercy on me and hear my prayer.

2   How long will you nobles dishonour my glory; ♦
how long will you love vain things and seek after falsehood?

3   But know that the Lord has shown me his marvellous kindness; ♦
when I call upon the Lord, he will hear me.

4   Stand in awe, and sin not; ♦
commune with your own heart upon your bed, and be still.

5   Offer the sacrifices of righteousness ♦
and put your trust in the Lord.

6   There are many that say, 'Who will show us any good?' ♦
Lord, lift up the light of your countenance upon us.

7　You have put gladness in my heart, ♦
　　more than when their corn and wine and oil increase.

8　In peace I will lie down and sleep, ♦
　　for it is you Lord, only, who make me dwell in safety.

Psalm 91

1　Whoever dwells in the shelter of the Most High ♦
　　and abides under the shadow of the Almighty,

2　Shall say to the Lord, 'My refuge and my stronghold, ♦
　　my God, in whom I put my trust.'

3　For he shall deliver you from the snare of the fowler ♦
　　and from the deadly pestilence.

4　He shall cover you with his wings
　　　　and you shall be safe under his feathers; ♦
　　his faithfulness shall be your shield and buckler.

5　You shall not be afraid of any terror by night, ♦
　　nor of the arrow that flies by day;

6　Of the pestilence that stalks in darkness, ♦
　　nor of the sickness that destroys at noonday.

7　Though a thousand fall at your side
　　　　and ten thousand at your right hand, ♦
　　yet it shall not come near you.

8　Your eyes have only to behold ♦
　　to see the reward of the wicked.

9　Because you have made the Lord your refuge ♦
　　and the Most High your stronghold,

10　There shall no evil happen to you, ♦
　　neither shall any plague come near your tent.

11　For he shall give his angels charge over you, ♦
　　to keep you in all your ways.

12　They shall bear you in their hands, ♦
　　lest you dash your foot against a stone.

13   You shall tread upon the lion and adder; ♦
      the young lion and the serpent you shall trample underfoot.

14   Because they have set their love upon me,
       therefore will I deliver them; ♦
      I will lift them up, because they know my name.

15   They will call upon me and I will answer them; ♦
      I am with them in trouble,
       I will deliver them and bring them to honour.

16   With long life will I satisfy them ♦
      and show them my salvation.

Psalm 134

1   Come, bless the Lord, all you servants of the Lord, ♦
      you that by night stand in the house of the Lord.

2   Lift up your hands towards the sanctuary ♦
      and bless the Lord.

3   The Lord who made heaven and earth ♦
      give you blessing out of Zion.

At the end of the psalmody, the following is said or sung

Glory to the Father and to the Son
and to the Holy Spirit;
as it was in the beginning is now
and shall be for ever. Amen.

One of the following short lessons or another suitable passage is read

You, O Lord, are in the midst of us and we are called by your name; leave us not, O Lord our God.   *Jeremiah 14.9*

(or)

Be sober, be vigilant, because your adversary the devil is prowling round like a roaring lion, seeking for someone to devour. Resist him, strong in the faith.   *1 Peter 5.8, 9*

(or)

The servants of the Lamb shall see the face of God, whose name will be on their foreheads. There will be no more night: they will not need the light of a lamp or the light of the sun, for God will be their light, and they will reign for ever and ever.   *Revelation 22.4, 5*

The following responsory may be said

Into your hands, O Lord, I commend my spirit.
All **Into your hands, O Lord, I commend my spirit.**
For you have redeemed me, Lord God of truth.
All **I commend my spirit.**
Glory to the Father, and to the Son, and to the Holy Spirit.
All **Into your hands, O Lord, I commend my spirit.**

Or, in Easter

Into your hands, O Lord, I commend my spirit.
　　Alleluia, alleluia.
All **Into your hands, O Lord, I commend my spirit.**
　　Alleluia, alleluia.
For you have redeemed me, Lord God of truth.
All **Alleluia, alleluia.**
Glory to the Father, and to the Son, and to the Holy Spirit.
All **Into your hands, O Lord, I commend my spirit.**
　　Alleluia, alleluia.

Keep me as the apple of your eye.
All **Hide me under the shadow of your wings.**

The Nunc dimittis (The Song of Simeon) is said or sung

All **Save us, O Lord, while waking,**
and guard us while sleeping,
that awake we may watch with Christ
and asleep may rest in peace.

1 Now, Lord, you let your servant go in peace: ♦
   your word has been fulfilled.

2 My own eyes have seen the salvation ♦
   which you have prepared in the sight of every people;

3 A light to reveal you to the nations ♦
   and the glory of your people Israel.   *Luke 2.29-32*

   Glory to the Father and to the Son
   and to the Holy Spirit;
   as it was in the beginning is now
   and shall be for ever. Amen.

All **Save us, O Lord, while waking,**
and guard us while sleeping,
that awake we may watch with Christ
and asleep may rest in peace.

Prayers

Intercessions and thanksgivings may be offered here.

The Collect

Silence may be kept.

Visit this place, O Lord, we pray,
and drive far from it the snares of the enemy;
may your holy angels dwell with us and guard us in peace,
and may your blessing be always upon us;
through Jesus Christ our Lord.

All **Amen.**

The Lord's Prayer may be said.

The Conclusion

In peace we will lie down and sleep;

All   **for you alone, Lord, make us dwell in safety.**

Abide with us, Lord Jesus,

All   **for the night is at hand and the day is now past.**

As the night watch looks for the morning,

All   **so do we look for you, O Christ.**

[Come with the dawning of the day

All   **and make yourself known in the breaking of the bread.**]

The Lord bless us and watch over us;
the Lord make his face shine upon us and be gracious to us;
the Lord look kindly on us and give us peace.

All   **Amen.**

Notes

1   Psalms

If it is desired to use an unchanging pattern of psalmody for Night Prayer, the psalms printed in the text are used. However, verses from other psalms may be used instead, particularly if Night Prayer is said daily – Saturday: as set; Sunday: Psalm 104; Monday: Psalm 86; Tuesday: Psalm 143; Wednesday: Psalm 31; Thursday: Psalm 16; Friday: Psalm 139.

2   Thanksgiving

Night Prayer may begin with the Prayer of Thanksgiving from Evening Prayer (page 40 in *Common Worship: Services and Prayers for the Church of England*).

3   Gospel Reading

On suitable occasions, particularly Saturday night and before other festivals, the Gospel for the following day may be read before the Office.

4   Preparation

When the confession is being used, it may be replaced by another act of penitence. However, all that precedes 'O God, make speed to save us' may be omitted; this is particularly appropriate if Holy Communion has been celebrated in the evening.

5   Alleluia

The Alleluias included in the Easter form of the Responsory are for use from Easter Day until the Day of Pentecost, not at other times. The Alleluia following the opening versicles and responses is always used, except in Lent.

6   The Conclusion

The response in square brackets [ ] is normally used only if Holy Communion is to be celebrated the following morning.

7   Seasons

The hymn, the Scripture reading, the refrain to the Gospel Canticle, the Collect and the blessing may change seasonally and on Festivals.

For General Rules for Regulating Authorized Forms of Service, see Common Worship: Services and Prayers for the Church of England *page 525.*

Authorization

The service and notes in this booklet have been commended by the House of Bishops of the General Synod pursuant to Canon B 2 of the Canons of the Church of England and are published with the agreement of the House.

Under Canon B 4 it is open to each bishop to authorize, if he sees fit, the form of service to be used within his diocese. He may specify that the services shall be those commended by the House, or that a diocesan form of them shall be used. If the bishop gives no directions in this matter the priest remains free, subject to the terms of Canon B 5, to make use of the material as commended by the House.

Acknowledgements

The publisher gratefully acknowledges permission to reproduce copyright material in this book. Every effort has been made to trace and contact copyright holders. If there are any inadvertent omissions we apologize to those concerned and undertake to include suitable acknowledgements in all future editions.

Published sources include the following:

The European Province of the Society of St Francis. Extracts adapted from *Celebrating Common Prayer* © The Society of St Francis European Province 1992 and 1996.